DOGS

by Sophie Geister-Jones

Cody Koala

An Imprint of Pop!
popbooksonline.com

abdobooks.com

Published by Pop!, a division of ABDO, PO Box 398166, Minneapolis, Minnesota 55439. Copyright © 2020 by POP, LLC. International copyrights reserved in all countries. No part of this book may be reproduced in any form without written permission from the publisher. Pop!™ is a trademark and logo of POP, LLC.

Printed in the United States of America, North Mankato, Minnesota

102019
012020

THIS BOOK CONTAINS RECYCLED MATERIALS

Cover Photo: iStockphoto
Interior Photos: iStockphoto, 1, 5 (top), 9, 18; Shutterstock Images, 5 (bottom left), 5 (bottom right), 6, 10–11, 13 (top), 13 (bottom left), 13 (bottom right), 14, 15, 17, 19, 20

Editor: Meg Gaertner
Series Designer: Sophie Geister-Jones

Library of Congress Control Number: 2019942762

Publisher's Cataloging-in-Publication Data

Names: Geister-Jones, Sophie, author
Title: Dogs / by Sophie Geister-Jones
Description: Minneapolis, Minnesota : Pop!, 2020 | Series: Pets | Includes online resources and index.
Identifiers: ISBN 9781532165696 (lib. bdg.) | ISBN 9781532167010 (ebook)
Subjects: LCSH: Dogs--Juvenile literature. | Dogs--Behavior--Juvenile literature. | Pets--Juvenile literature. | Domestic dog--Juvenile literature.
Classification: DDC 636.7--dc23

Hello! My name is
Cody Koala

Pop open this book and you'll find QR codes like this one, loaded with information, so you can learn even more!

Scan this code* and others like it while you read, or visit the website below to make this book pop.

popbooksonline.com/dogs

*Scanning QR codes requires a web-enabled smart device with a QR code reader app and a camera.

Table of Contents

Chapter 1
Behavior 4

Chapter 2
History. 8

Chapter 3
Many Types of Dogs . . . 12

Chapter 4
Dog Care 16

Making Connections 22
Glossary. 23
Index 24
Online Resources 24

Behavior

Dogs are active animals. They run. They chew bones. Some dogs play fetch. An owner throws a stick or a ball. The dog chases it and brings it back to the owner.

Watch a video here!

Dogs move their tails to show how they are feeling. A low tail between the legs can mean fear. A tail **wagging** from side to side can mean friendliness.

A dog's sense of smell is 10,000 to 100,000 times stronger than a human's.

Chapter 2

History

Humans have lived with dogs for thousands of years. At first, dogs kept people safe from other animals. They helped hunters find **prey**.

Learn more here!

Some groups of people used dogs for travel. Teams of dogs pulled sleds across snow. Sleds carried people.

Some held supplies too. Over time, people began keeping dogs as **companions**.

People in some snowy areas continue to go dog sledding.

Chapter 3

Many Types of Dogs

Today, there are more than 400 **breeds** of dogs. Different breeds have different needs. People should choose their dogs carefully.

Learn more here!

Dogs come in many different colors and sizes. Some breeds are small. Some do not have any hair.

Other breeds are large
and fluffy.

Just as each person's fingerprints are
unique, no two dogs have the same
noseprint.

Chapter 4

Dog Care

Dogs eat meat, fruit, grains, and vegetables. Most dogs get these foods in **kibble**. A **vet** can help owners decide on the right food for their dogs.

Complete an activity here!

Dogs sometimes get
dirty and smelly. Owners
should give their dogs baths.

Owners should also brush
their dogs' fur. Brushing
keeps dogs' fur healthy.

Dogs need to exercise. Owners can go on walks with their dogs. They can also go to dog parks. In these parks, dogs can run and play with one another.

Making Connections

Text-to-Self

Have you ever seen a dog play? What was it doing?

Text-to-Text

Have you read other books about pets? How is taking care of a dog similar to or different from caring for other animals?

Text-to-World

Why do you think people enjoy having dogs as companions?

Glossary

breed – a group of animals that all look similar.

companion – a person or animal that is friendly and spends time with another person or animal.

kibble – a dry food that dogs eat.

prey – an animal that is hunted, caught, or eaten by another animal.

vet – a doctor who takes care of animals.

wag – to move quickly back and forth.

Index

bones, 4

breeds, 12, 14–15

companions, 11

food, 16

sleds, 10

smell, 7

tails, 6, 7

vet, 16

Online Resources

popbooksonline.com

Thanks for reading this Cody Koala book!

Scan this code* and others like it in this book, or visit the website below to make this book pop!

popbooksonline.com/dogs

*Scanning QR codes requires a web-enabled smart device with a QR code reader app and a camera.